# 100 CUPS OF
# *compassion*

## Robin Hamman

Copyright © 2021 ROBIN HAMMAN
Published by Two Penny Publishing
850 E. Lime Street, #266 Tarpon Springs, Florida 34698
TwoPennyPublishing.com

THE HOLY BIBLE, NEW INTERNATIONAL VERSION®, NIV®
Copyright © 1973, 1978, 1984, 2011 by Biblica, Inc.™
Used by permission.

All Rights Reserved. No part of this publication may be reproduced, stored in a retrieval system, or transmitted, in any form or by any means, electronic, mechanical, photocopying, recording, or otherwise, without the prior written permission of Robin Hamman.

For permission requests and ordering information, contact Robin Hamman:
ArtRobStudios@gmail.com

Cover Design: Emily Montes de Oca


Printed in the United States of America.
ISBN 978-1-950995-41-7

# *endorsement*

I've had the pleasure of knowing Robin for more than ten years. She is a gifted artist with a caring heart full of compassion for people and pets. To know Robin is to love her. Besides being a fantastic artist, she has a quick wit and a radiant smile that can brighten any day. Her book, 100 Cups of Compassion, offers a glimpse into her love for God and undeniable passion for a colorful life.

Knowing each painting has a story of its own made my journey through this journal a more intimate experience.

I recommend a cup of tea while you engage with this treasure. Steep yourself into each message, journal notes to yourself. Just know that Robin has put a piece of her soul into this that will linger in your heart forever.

**Valerie Jane Wilson**
Certified Life Coach, Writer, Speaker
HopeDefinedMe.com

I dedicate this book to every person in this world
struggling with addiction.
Whether you are sober, struggling, strung out, in
your millionth rehab stay, homeless,
sick, lost, broken, bent, angry or you think you
are too far gone to be saved,

*please hold on*

God Loves You! It is the TRUTH.
I love you, too.

# *introduction*

For decades, I have been creating little paintings or doodles of coffee and or teacups. They started out so organically as a way to loosen up my brush strokes when I was painting something complicated like a human being. The doodles evolved into a massive body of work that always left me asking, "What are these things and where are they coming from?" They just kept coming! I kept painting them.

Community and compassion. Those two words became the foundation for these cup paintings. In the beginning, I would sit for hours in coffee shops around Florida and paint. If I heard of someone having a bad day I would give them a painting. I would also blog about the experience. As my blog went out into the world, people would contact me, to inquire about acquiring a painting. I always responded, but being

compassionate did not always come easy. I, as a human, grappled with taking one of my creations and just handing it over to a complete stranger. I put several hours of my time and energy into these paintings and in some cases, because of pride, I simply didn't want to GIVE them away! What if my creation ended up in a garbage can or worse, a garage sale!? This is when I would hear God speaking to me about the Fruit of the Spirit in Galatians 5. God was revealing to me that my pride was causing me to not share the gift and talent that he had given me.

I believe God breathed life into these paintings and I believe it is his direction leading me to and through the creative process. Each painting was painted with love, pain, sadness, happiness, struggle and frustration. They have found homes all around the world-- from Tunisia to Cuba to Mexico and all across this beautiful country. They are meant to brighten someone's day, to uplift and to encourage. Each one of these paintings picked its current owners. At least that is the way it usually happens. I hope you enjoy this little book, read some of God's words, write in it, paint in it, create with it and share it with friends and family.

Connect with me:

Facebook.com/100cupsofcompassion

Instagram.com/100cups

Instagram.com/artrobstudios

100CupsOfCompassion.com

thetwistedleash.com

Artrobstudios.com

*Robin Hammar*

artist 100cupsofcompassion

Previously known as *Robin Borland*

# give thanks

Praise and Glory to God!
Thank you, **Ollie**, for being my son. I love you!
You inspire me more than you will ever know.

To my family and friends that stuck with me through some pretty black days.

My husband **Larry** (Lar-bear).
My sister, **Wendy**.
My **Mary Jo**.
The **Cuzins**.

**Valerie**: HopeDefinedMe.com

**Juanita, Rob** and my **HW Davis family!**
The **Washington Street Wanderers** and all of the Washington St. crew.

All of you at **TARC**, who struggle with addiction every day. You are an inspiration.

**Michelle and Gary,** my life long friends.

**Two Sparrows:** ShopTwoSparrows.com for allowing me to use their cool bags for my collages.

**Maribel** for creating such wonderful artwork on those cool bags.

Cheers **Emily Montes de Oca**! You have always branded me well!

**Jodi** at Two Penny Publishing for your patience and guidance.

# Deuteronomy 31:6

Be strong and courageous.

Do not be afraid or terrified because of them for the Lord your God goes with you.

He will never leave you or forsake you.

# NOTES

_____
_____
_____
_____
_____
_____
_____
_____
_____
_____
_____
_____

Sometimes life finds us in places that are dark and very hard to see our way out of, but God tells us not to be afraid. Get up, Keep moving forward! He is with you. He will never leave you or forsake you.

*It is a promise!*

*He's got the whole world in His hands*

My friend, Amy, is a missionary in North Africa. She requested a cup with the world painted on it and I was happy to oblige. She turned my paintings into postcards she gives to friends!

# NOTES

This is my first cup painting after two rough years in my life. My 23-year marriage came to an end. I had loved ones suffering through addiction. I was being treated for breast cancer. Everything hitting me at one time left me lost. I was tired mentally, physically and spiritually beyond anything I had ever experienced. Things didn't turn out the way I thought they would.

I prayed fiercely for God to show up and fix the problems. God did show up. He healed me in many ways and although things did not always turn out as I had hoped they might, there was healing. In this artwork, the crack in the cup has been made lovely by a row of diamonds. Cracks symbolically appear in many of the cups I have painted after that time in my life. They are a reminder that we might be chipped or cracked, but God sees us as beautiful!

# NOTES

> *There is a crack in everything, that's how the light gets in.*
> – Leonard Cohen

### 1 John 4:7

*Beloved*, let us love one another
for love is of God,
and whoever loves has been
born of God
and knows God.

# NOTES

I love coffee! For centuries, coffee and tea have been bringing people together. The cups I paint symbolize safety and comfort, unity, warmth, togetherness and oneness of the human race. Over tea and coffee, we share life's ups, downs and unexpected happenings. We all have our favorite coffee or teacup. What's yours?

## Philippians 4:8

Finally, brethren, whatever things are true, whatever things are honest, whatever things are just, whatever things are pure, whatever things are lovely, whatever things are of good report; if there be any virtue, and if there be any praise, think on these things.

## NOTES

_____
_____
_____
_____
_____
_____
_____
_____
_____
_____
_____
_____
_____
_____
_____
_____
_____

## *What to Think About*

Do you ever find yourself thinking about all of the chaos in the world and then realizing you have become angry or sad or unfocused?

The Bible tells us where to focus our attention.

# Joy

*I love that word.
It even sounds fun*

# NOTES

## Psalm 100:2

Worship the Lord with gladness; come before him with *joyful* songs.

two

# NOTES

*May you trust
God that you
are exactly
where you
are meant
to be.*

— St. Terese of Lisieux

*We were all born with the ability to create.*
~ Robin Hamman

# NOTES

_____
_____
_____
_____
_____
_____
_____
_____
_____
_____
_____
_____
_____
_____
_____

Being creative doesn't always mean being an artist. Anyone can use their imagination to problem solve, overcome life challenges or just check out for a while and take a mental vacation. Praying, sitting in stillness talking to God, inviting the Holy Spirit into your thoughts and actions and every crevice of your life is also a form of creativity. Creating with the one who created EVERYTHING: THAT is a great way to be creative!

# MY CUP OVERFLOWS

**Psalm 23:5-6**

You prepare a table before me in the presence of my enemies.

You anoint my head with oil; my cup overflows.

Surely your goodness and love will follow me all the days of my life, and I will dwell in the house of the Lord *forever.*

# NOTES

There are so many small blessings in life that can make even the darkest days a little *brighter*.
Fresh air, a sunrise, a sunset, or finding a quiet place to be still for a few moments to pray and talk to God. Look for the small blessing and your cup will overflow.

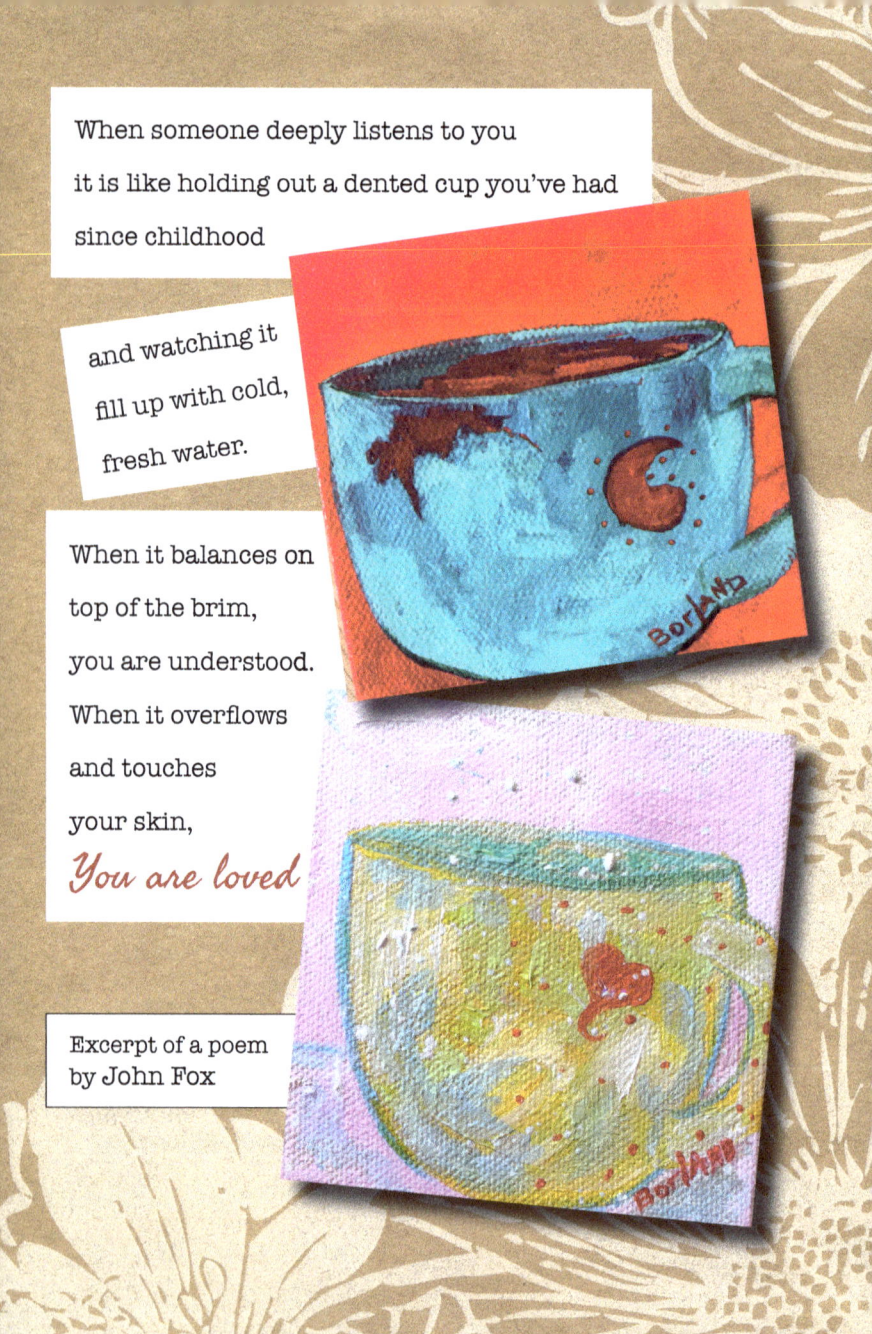

When someone deeply listens to you
it is like holding out a dented cup you've had
since childhood

and watching it
fill up with cold,
fresh water.

When it balances on
top of the brim,
you are understood.
When it overflows
and touches
your skin,
*You are loved*

Excerpt of a poem
by John Fox

# NOTES

**Mark 4:39**

He got up, rebuked the wind and said to the waves, 'Quiet! Be still!' Then the wind died down and it was completely calm.

# NOTES

*Quiet.*
*Be still.*
*Rest.*

When I researched the word rest, as it pertains to the Bible, I found that it does not necessarily mean to stop doing what you are doing or to sleep. No, it simply means to come into God's order of things. There is a natural, God created, order to life. God is inviting you to bring your life into his order of things and there you will find "rest."

The Paw Print cups were given to friends who are animal lovers, animal rescues and people who just love their furry friends!

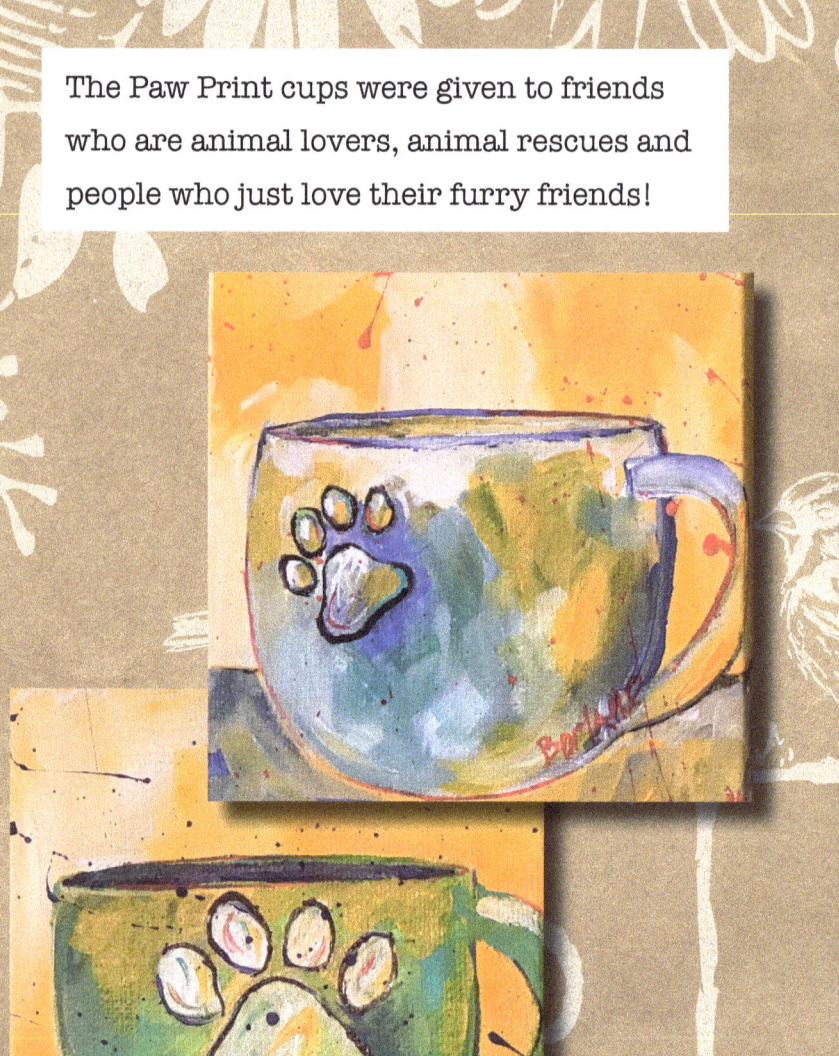

# NOTES

If you have men who will exclude any of God's creatures from the shelter of compassion and pity, you will have men who will deal likewise with their fellow men.
- St. Francis of Assisi

## Psalms 121:7-8

The Lord will keep you from all harm—he will watch over your life; the Lord will watch over your coming and going both now and forevermore.

# NOTES

These cups often find their way onto other surfaces and substances besides canvas. They, too, get bored, lost, and wander away from their original path just like us.

# NOTES

---
---
---
---
---
---
---
---
---
---
---

## Luke 15:3-7

Now the tax collectors and sinners were all
gathering around to hear Jesus.
Then Jesus told them this parable:
"Suppose one of you has a hundred sheep and loses one of them.
Doesn't he leave the ninety-nine in the open country and
go after the lost sheep until he finds it?
And when he finds it, he joyfully puts it on his shoulders
and goes home. Then he calls his friends and neighbors together
and says, 'Rejoice with me; I have found my lost sheep.'
I tell you that in the same way there will be more rejoicing in
heaven over one sinner who repents than over ninety-nine
righteous persons who do not need to repent.

Don't allow any sadness to dwell in your soul, for sadness prevents the Holy Spirit from acting freely.

— St. Pio of Pietrelcina

# NOTES

> "Pray, hope, and don't worry. Worry is useless. God is merciful and will hear your prayer."
>
> - Padre Pio

### Hebrews 6:19

We have this *hope* as an anchor for the soul, firm and secure. It enters the inner sanctuary behind the curtain." Christ is our hope. Always with us, never changing.

# NOTES

"Darkness can not drive out darkness; only light can do that"

This is an original quote by Dr. Martin Luther King, Jr. God decided it belonged in my fortune cookie one night!

# NOTES

_____
_____
_____
_____
_____
_____
_____
_____
_____
_____
_____
_____
_____
_____
_____   _____

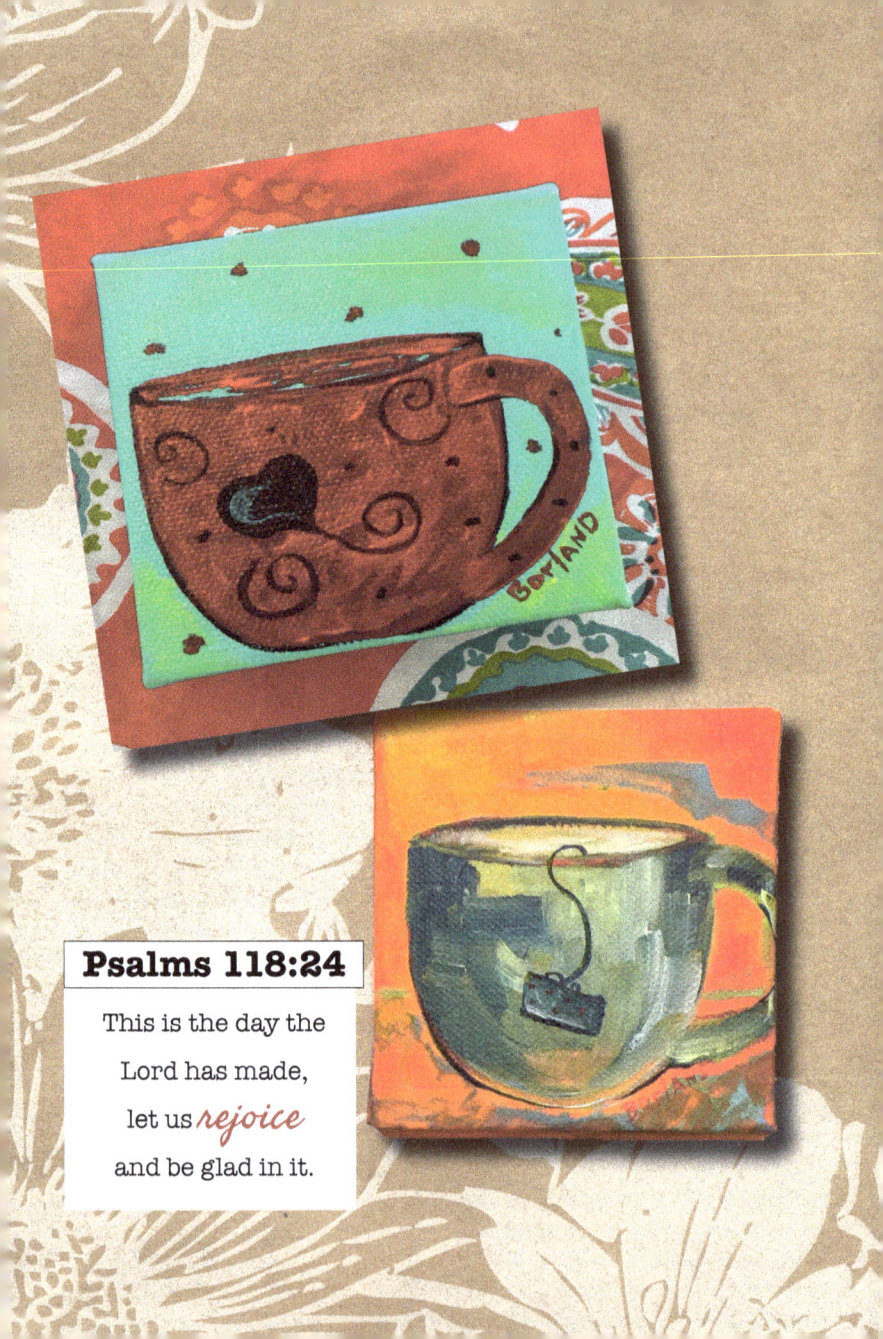

**Psalms 118:24**

This is the day the Lord has made, let us *rejoice* and be glad in it.

# NOTES

This was one of my Grandma Hamman's favorite Bible verses. She had a sticker stuck to a bathroom tile with this passage written on it. I grew up reading that sticker whenever I would visit her. God can surely reach you anywhere you are. He works in mysterious ways!

# Ask, Seek, Knock

## Revelation 3:20

"Here I am! I stand at the door and knock. If anyone hears my voice and opens the door, I will come in and eat with that person, and they with me."

## Matthew 7:7-8

Ask, and it will be given to you; search, and you will find; knock, and the door will be opened for you.
For everyone who asks receives, and everyone who searches finds, and for everyone who knocks, the door will be opened.

# NOTES

*The invitation could not be any clearer. All are welcome!*

# NOTES

### Exodus 13:21-22

By day the Lord went ahead of them in a pillar of cloud to guide them on their way and by night in a pillar of fire to give them light, so that they could travel by day or night. Neither the pillar of cloud by day nor the pillar of fire by night left its place in front of the people.

# NOTES

*The Lord is always with you*

# God is always with you!

**Psalms 16:11**

You show me the path of life. In your presence there is fullness of joy; in your right hand are pleasures forevermore.

# NOTES

*Jesus said he is the Way, the Truth and the Life. He will always show you the way.*

We are all looking for peace in our lives. Everyone wants security, comfort and a smooth path, but the only real way to achieve those things is through the Love of Christ. His *peace* "transcends all understanding…" He will guard your heart and your mind. It is his promise.

## Philippians 4:6-7

Do not be anxious about anything, but in every situation, by prayer and petition, with thanksgiving, present your requests to God. And the peace of God, which transcends all understanding, will guard your hearts and your minds in Christ Jesus.

# NOTES

# Trust Him!

## Isaiah 42:16

I will turn the darkness before them into light,
the rough places into level ground.

# NOTES

Just think about what God is doing for you right now! Even in the dark places, he wants you to know that he will turn those dark places into *light.*

## Peace Prayer of St Francis

Lord, make me an instrument of your peace:
where there is hatred, let me sow love;
where there is injury, pardon; where there is doubt, faith;
where there is despair, hope; where there is darkness, light;
where there is sadness, joy.
O divine Master, grant that I may not so much seek
to be consoled as to console,
to be understood as to understand, to be loved as to love.
For it is in giving that we receive,
it is in pardoning that we are pardoned,
and it is in dying that we are born to eternal life.

Amen.

# NOTES

### Serenity Prayer

God grant me the serenity to accept the things I cannot change;
courage to change the things I can;
and wisdom to know the difference.
Living one day at a time; enjoying one moment at a time;
accepting hardships as the pathway to peace;
taking, as He did, this sinful world as it is, not as I would have it;
trusting that He will make all things right if I surrender to His Will;
that I may be reasonably happy in this life
and supremely happy with Him forever in the next.
Amen.

Reinhold Niebuhr (1892-1971)

# NOTES

It's a slow night in the backyard,
just you and me the dogs and the stars...

song lyrics by Wendy Drexler

## Isaiah 55:8-9

"For my thoughts are not your thoughts, neither are your ways my ways," declares the Lord. "As the heavens are higher than the earth, so are my ways higher than your ways and my thoughts than your thoughts."

# NOTES

## *Trust God*

We don't have the full picture, our stories are being written and are continuous. God has the answers and we don't. It is for this reason we must trust him and "lean not on our own understanding"

## Isaiah 43:1-3

But now, this is what the Lord says—he who created you,
Jacob, he who formed you, Israel:
"Do not fear, for I have redeemed you;
I have summoned you by name; you are mine.
When you pass through the waters, I will be with you;
and when you pass through the rivers,
they will not sweep over you.
When you walk through the fire, you will not be burned;
the flames will not set you ablaze.
For I am the Lord your God,
the Holy One of Israel, your Savior.

# NOTES

When you lose a *loved one* it leaves a hole in your life.

So often people try to fill that void with things. Sometimes those things can be destructive, like drugs or alcohol. The apostle Paul addresses this in the Bible:

1 Thessalonians 4:13 "Now concerning those who have fallen asleep: we don't want you to remain in ignorance about them, my dear family. We don't want you to have the kind of grief that other people do, people who don't have any hope."

# NOTES

_____
_____
_____
_____
_____
_____
_____
_____
_____
_____
_____
_____
_____
_____
_____

**We have *hope* that we will be united again with those that we have lost.**

**Exodus 14:14**

"The Lord will fight for you, you need only to be still"

# NOTES

_____
_____
_____
_____
_____
_____
_____
_____
_____
_____
_____
_____
_____

Think about this: The God who made heaven and earth, and all that is in it, fights for you! He tells you you need "only to be still"! How wonderful is that! We seem to fight so hard to make things right or for physical or mental healing, but God's got this! He will slay the dragons!

You only need to *Be Still.*

## 2 Corinthians 4:8-10

"We are hard-pressed on every side, but not crushed; perplexed, but not in despair; persecuted, but not abandoned; struck down, but not destroyed. We always carry around in our body the death of Jesus, so that the life of Jesus may also be revealed in our body."

# NOTES

**1 Peter:3:15**

"Through thick and thin, keep your hearts at attention,

in adoration before Christ, your Master.

Be ready to speak up and tell anyone who asks why you're living the way you are, and always with the utmost courtesy."

# NOTES

**James 1:19-20**

My dear brothers and sisters, take note of this: Everyone should be quick to listen, slow to speak and slow to become angry, because human anger does not produce the righteousness that God desires."

# NOTES

_____
_____
_____
_____
_____
_____
_____

_____
_____
_____
_____
_____
_____
_____
_____
_____

> In prayer, more is accomplished by *listening* than by talking. Let us leave to God the decisions as to what shall be said.
>
> - St. Frances of De Sales

**Psalms 121:1**

"I lift up my eyes to the mountains—
where does my help come from?
My help comes from the Lord,
the Maker of heaven and earth."

# NOTES

_____

_____

_____

_____

_____

_____

_____

_____

_____

_____

_____

_____

_____

**2 Samuel 22:4**

"I called to the LORD, who is worthy of praise, and have been *saved* from my enemies."

**Psalms 121: 7-8**

"The Lord will keep you from all harm—
he will watch over your life;
the Lord will watch over your coming
and going both now and forevermore."

# NOTES

**Psalms 139:13**

"For you created my inmost being; you knit me together in my mother's womb."

# NOTES

> "I have a Creator who knew all things, even before they were made. Even me, his poor little child."
>
> - St. Patrick

## Ephesians 3:20-21

"Now to him who is able to do immeasurably more than all we ask or imagine, according to his *power* that is at work within us, to him be glory in the church and in Christ Jesus throughout all generations, forever and ever!" Amen.

# NOTES

## 1 Peter 1:13

Therefore, with minds that are alert and fully sober set your *hope* on the grace to be brought to you when Jesus Christ is revealed at his coming.

# NOTES

When *100 Cups* began to reach over the country via social media, someone contacted me from Oregon who was devastated by *The Umpqua Community College* shooting that occurred on October 1, 2015, near Roseburg, Oregon.

This person requested a painted cup with a heart over the town in Oregon that was hurting so badly from this horrific event. In remembrance of the victims, I wrote their names on the back of the painting.

# NOTES

**Psalms 34:18**

The Lord is close to the brokenhearted and saves those who are crushed in spirit.

## Ephesians 3: 16-21

I pray that out of his glorious riches he may strengthen
you with power through his Spirit in your inner being,
so that Christ may dwell in your hearts through faith.
And I pray that you, being rooted and established in love,
may have power, together with all the Lord's holy people,
to grasp how wide and long and high and deep is the love of Christ,
and to know this love that surpasses knowledge—
that you may be filled to the measure of all the fullness of God.

# NOTES

## Psalms 91:1

Whoever dwells in the shelter of the Most High will rest in the shadow of the *Almighty.*

# NOTES

### **Proverbs 3:5-6**

Trust in the Lord with all your *heart*
and lean not on your own understanding;
in all your ways submit to Him,
and He will make your paths straight.

# NOTES

# Isaiah 54:17

No weapon formed against you shall prosper, and every tongue which rises against you in judgment You shall condemn. This is the heritage of the servants of the Lord, and their righteousness is from Me," says the Lord.

# NOTES

## 1 Corinthians 10:13

No temptation has overtaken you except
what is common to mankind.

*And God is faithful;*
he will not let you be tempted
beyond what you can bear.
But when you are tempted,
he will also provide a way out
so that you can endure it.

# NOTES

**Psalms 119:36**

Turn my heart toward your statutes

and not toward selfish gain.

# NOTES

So often we turn to everything and everyone around us to make us happy but true happiness can only be found through a relationship with the Father, Son and Holy Spirit.

# NOTES

**Psalms 40:4**

Blessed is the one who trusts in the Lord,
who does not look to the proud,
to those who turn aside to false gods

My home, St. Augustine, Florida, is the oldest city in the United States. In 2015, the city celebrated its 450th birthday. When Pedro Menendez discovered this land it was on the feast day of St Augustine. St Augustine committed every sin known to man and through the prayers of his mother, had a conversion and a deep profound love of God and Christ. He went on to become a Doctor of the Catholic Church.

# NOTES

> Hope has two beautiful daughters. Their names are Anger and Courage: Anger at the way things are, and Courage to see that they do not remain the way they are.
>
> St. Augustine

NOTES

**Revelations 8:4**

The smoke of the incense along with the prayers of the holy ones went up before God from the hand of the angel.

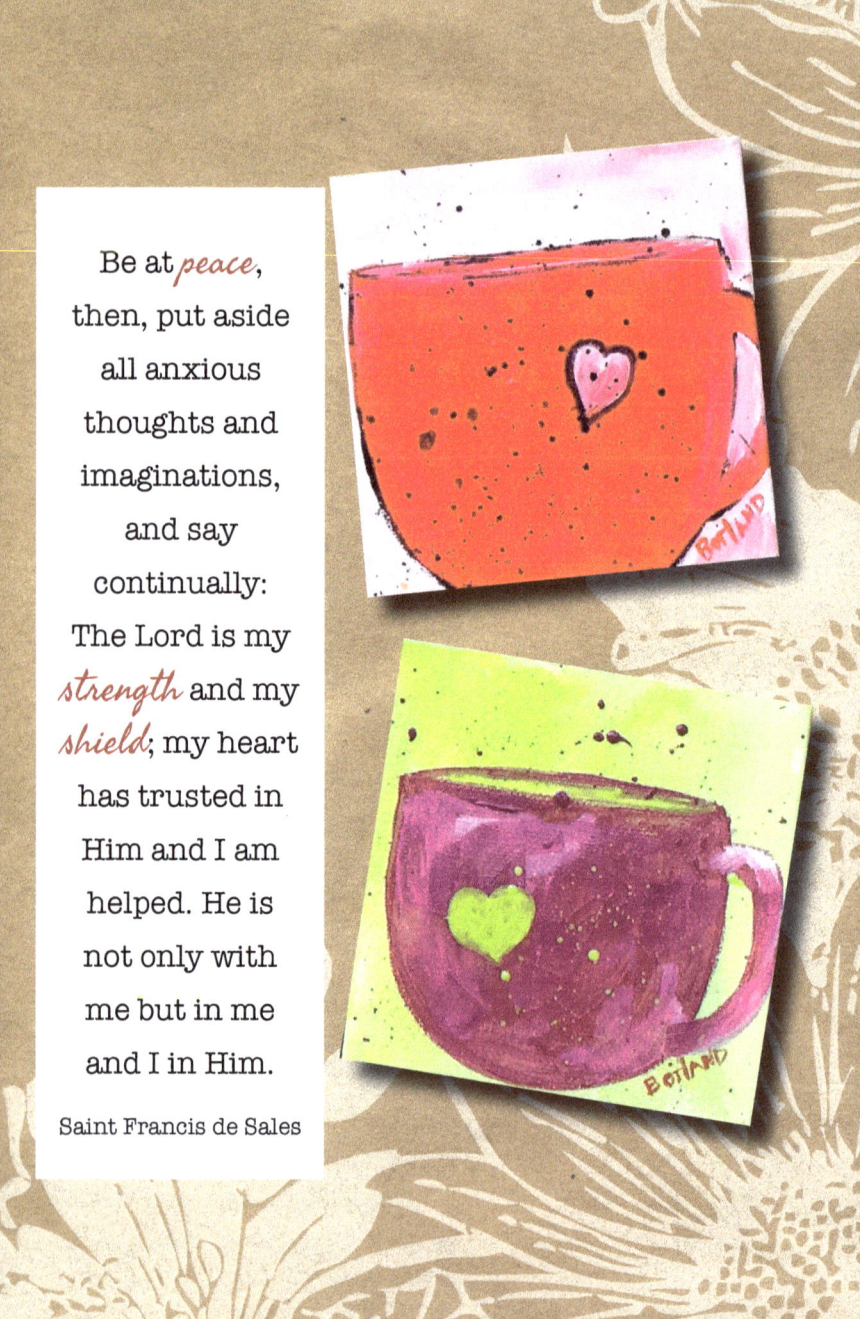

Be at *peace*, then, put aside all anxious thoughts and imaginations, and say continually: The Lord is my *strength* and my *shield*; my heart has trusted in Him and I am helped. He is not only with me but in me and I in Him.

Saint Francis de Sales

# NOTES

*Live in faith and hope,*
though it be in darkness,
for in this darkness God protects the soul.
Cast your care upon God for you are His
and He will not forget you.
Do not think that He is leaving you alone,
for that would be to wrong Him.

– St. John of the Cross

# NOTES

## Ephesians 6:16

In all circumstances take up the shield of faith, with which you can extinguish all the flaming darts of the evil one.

# NOTES

**John 3:16-17**

For God so *loved* the world,
that he gave his only Son,
that whoever believes in him
should not perish but have eternal life.

For God did not send his Son into the world
to condemn the world,
but in order that the world might
be *saved* through him.

# NOTES

*Sometimes we all just need this reminder.*

*Have faith.*

# about the author

## ROBIN HAMMAN

Robin received her degree in Fine Art from the University of South Florida and her Masters degree in Arts In Medicine from the University of Florida. She began her full-time career painting at a studio in Dunedin Florida in 1999. Robin helped to create and manage *Trailside Artist Colony*, an artist co-op dedicated to helping professional artists show, market and sell their work.

In 2000, Robin moved her studio into her home in Safety Harbor Florida and began a career in local politics as a commissioner for the city of Safety Harbor.

Robin continued her painting throughout her political career often painting places that she would visit on vacation or business. "I like to capture places and people as they are in that moment in time. I try to convey not only what my eye is seeing, but also what emotions are being felt by the people or places in that moment in time." I paint quickly trying to get down every feeling that I have as I experience it" "I use color, line, and shape to build images that will project an emotion to the person viewing the art."

Robin works in acrylic as well as oil. She has worked with veterans in recovery at a program she designed called *Veterans Creating for Community*. She has also worked with seniors and kids with substance addictions. "Art making can distract from issues that a person may have, helping to promote a peaceful mind as well as enhance positive mental and physical outcomes."

Along with working in the Arts In Medicine field, Robin has also launched an *Art In Compassion* initiative entitled *100 Cups of Compassion* and a pet portrait business called *The Twisted Leash*. Her work can also be found at *ArtRobStudios*, her online gallery where she offers online classes, artist retreats and sells her work. She resides in St Augustine, Florida.

www.ingramcontent.com/pod-product-compliance
Lightning Source LLC
Chambersburg PA
CBHW041325110526
44592CB00021B/2828